EXTREME

POSITIONS

S

s s s s
s s s s
s s s s

EXTREME POSITIONS

bpNichol

s s s s s s s s
s s s s s s s
s s s s s s s s
s s s s s s s
s s s s s s s s
s s s s s s s

for Frank & Linda Davey

"a murmer mystery"

s s s s s s s s s s s s
s s s s s s s s s s s
s s s s s s s s s s s s
s s s s s s s s s s s
s s s s s s s s s s s s
s s s s s s s s s s s
s s s s s s s s s s s s
s s s s s s s s s s s
s s s s s s s s s s s s

two
wives
wove
two
waves

twice
wined
twice
wifed

two
waves
woven

two
wives

s s s s s s s s s s s s s s s s
s s s s s s s s s s s s s s s s
s s s s s s s s s s s s s s s s
s s s s s s s s s s s s s s s s
s s s s s s s s s s s s s s s s
s s s s s s s s s s s s s s s s
s s s s s s s s s s s s s s s s
s s s s s s s s s s s s s s s s
s s s s s s s s s s s s s s s s
s s s s s s s s s s s s s s s s
s s s s s s s s s s s s s s s s
s s s s s s s s s s s s s s s s
s s s s s s s s s s s s s s s s

s s s s s s s s s s s s s s s s s s s s
s s s s s s s s s s s s s s s s s s s s
s s s s s s s s s s s s s s s s s s s s
s s s s s s s s s s s s s s s s s s s s
s s s s s s s s s s s s s s s s s s s s
s s s s s s s s s s s s s s s s s s s s
s s s s s s s s s s s s s s s s s s s s
s s s s s s s s s s s s s s s s s s s s
s s s s s s s s s s s s s s s s s s s s
s s s s s s s s s s s s s s s s s s s s
s s s s s s s s s s s s s s s s s s s s
s s s s s s s s s s s s s s s s s s s s
s s s s s s s s s s s s s s s s s s s s
s s s s s s s s s s s s s s s s s s s s
s s s s s s s s s s s s s s s s s s s s
s s s s s s s s s s s s s s s s s s s s

1

moon

owl

tree

path or road

stand ing

tree

tree

tree

birds

moon

opening

hand

landing

star

star

cloud

land

lake

wind

wave

hand

wave

boat

empty

cloud

cloud

cloud

water

light

lake

tree

bush

road me

bush

brush

sky

him

step house

field

window

picture

chair

you

her

eye

moon

tree

(adow)

shh

lake

wave

shore

sky

landing

boat

face

tree

table

chair

empty

2

moving

runs

sitting

scream

crying

laughs

will SHOUT

didn't SHOUT

should SHOUT

can't SHOUT

smile

gestures

stands up

looking

rowing

waves

laughing

smiles

sitting down

sat

cries or
(smile?)
wishes

for
get

for
got

3

yesterday’s

colourful

bright

vio
lent
let

swift

bloody

vague

(ness
(ly
))

frighten

startled

(
ah)

(ha
zy)

4

running or sitting or
running while sitting or
running remembering sitting or
yes

            everything at once
altogether
completely tangled up

rowing or sitting or
rowing while sitting or
rowing remembering
no

            everything at once
altogether & forgotten
completely remembered
thrown out

sitting laughing

to sit & laugh

hands

laughing & sitting

seated laughing

hands

sitting & laughing &
laughing & laughing &
laughing & laughing &
seated laughing

laughing

will shout

(shouts)

didn't shout

(shouted)

can't shout

(wants to shout)

shouts out

(should shout)

shh

wave

wave

wave

boat

wave

wave

wave

wave

happy & sad laughing
remembered laughing hysterical

hysterical sad laughing &
remembered laughing happy

waves

remembered laughing laughing &
sad hysterical happy

remembered & hysterical
laughing laughing
                                        happy
                                                    sad

sitting or standing
standing or
sitting
sitting or
standing
                    gestures &

sitting

sitting or
standing or
standing sitting or
sitting standing &

                                   gestures

the bright boat in
the bright sun on
the bright water in
the bright light in
the eye

in the light
in the water
in the sun
in the boat in
the bright bright bright bright

table fork table plate table knife table

moon or sun

sun’s moon

ing sunny &

moon’s sun

sun’s moon

y sunning &

moon’s sun

sun or moon

table plate sun fork table knife plate table moon

shadowy shadow
shadowed shadowing
shadows shade
shedding
            shed
shys
      shaded
shift

road
lake
road
road
lake
road
road
road
lake
road
road
road
road
lake
rowing

5

why

why not

not why
but why
but not why
not why not but why

why & how

how why

but how
not why

not how but why

how why but not how

how & why

three
of them
of two of
us &
two
them
of us of them

two

three

no

        yes

no
no

        yes
        yes

no
no
no

        yes
        yes
        yes

noyes

noise

an accusation

accusing

(accused)

accustomed as

"unaccustomed as"

accusatory

(a customary)

costumed

accusingly

consuming

runs

stops

runs & runs

stops

runs & runs & runs

stops

runs & runs & runs & runs

stops

stops

oon

like a lock a lac un like a luck y leak a lack a lake

m

grieving

stands by the lake
sits at the table
walks down the road
runs down the road
gets up from the table
stands in the lake
rows the boat
rows the boa
rows the bo
rows the b
rows the
ows the
ws the
s the
the
th
t

hand

wave

head

wave

hand

wave

wave

wave

head

wave

wave

wave

wave

wave

wave

wave

the moon rises

the moon sets

the sun rises

the sun sets

the moon rises

the sun rises

the moon sets

the sun sets

back.

back & forth &

rocking.

forth &

rock.

lake.

ing.

row.

& back &
forth forth.
back & back &
back & forth &
back.
back.

6

two
    times
two
        two twos

time

two twos
to two

(to

everything multiplied
once by itself
multiplied itself by everything
one multiple
everything

by itself

pardon me pardon
me pardon me

yes

me forgive me
forgive me forgive

yes

you can you
can you can

yes

thank you thank
you thank you

  a
l a k e
  a
l a n e
  a
l i n e
  a
l o n e

```
    a
w  av  e
    a
weav  e
 e  v  e  ning
          nin  e
w  av  es
    a
weav       ing
```

boat afloat
like a lake
like an empty lake
        an empty boat
afloat

wave
wave wave
wave wife wave
wave wave wave wave
wave wavewave wave
wavee wavweave wwave
wave wawvaeve wave
wwavve wwaavvee wwavee
wave wwaavvee wave
waave wawvaeve wavve
wave wavweave wave
wwave wavewave wavee
wave wave wave wave
wave wife wave
wave wave
wave

waves

S

e

ISBN 0-919285-07-4

Typesetting and layout: Marni L. Stanley

THE LONGSPOON PRESS
c/o Dept. of English
University of Alberta
Edmonton, Alberta
T6G 2E5

Longspoon Press is a mail order press.
Books should be ordered directly from the publisher.

Longspoon Press wishes gratefully to acknowledge financial assistance for the publication of *extreme positions* from the following:

ALBERTA CULTURE, Film and Literary Arts Branch
THE CANADA COUNCIL
THE UNIVERSITY OF ALBERTA ENDOWMENT FUND FOR THE FUTURE, University/Community Special Projects Fund